as if a caress

New and Selected Poems

j.lewis

ISBN: 978-81-8253-910-5

First Edition: 2022

Rs. 200/-

Cyberwit.net

HIG 45 Kaushambi Kunj, Kalindipuram

Allahabad - 211011 (U.P.) India

http://www.cyberwit.net

Tel: +(91) 9415091004

E-mail: info@cyberwit.net

Printed at VCORRE PRESS.

Dedication

This book is dedicated to the many people who have touched my life in positive ways.

Special thanks to Jeannie E. Roberts for the line that inspired both the title of this collection and the poem of the same name.

FOREWORD

In a world where harshness, violence, and isolation abound, a caress can be the single most surprising and appreciated gesture. I use the term caress to mean basically any gentle contact made with a hand. This can be a hand on a shoulder, a pat or a rub on the back, a stroke on an arm, laying your hand on another hand, or brushing a cheek. It may occur as we laugh together, cry together, or work together. It is one of the most basic and natural gestures between people.

This type of contact is affirmational. It says to the person who is caressed "You exist. I see you. I value you. You matter."

Experiences with nature may produce a different type of caress – a soft autumn breeze, sunsets, the whispering of the wind in a forest, watching deer quietly grazing. There is no hand touching us, but we are moved by them nonetheless.

Spoken and written words can convey to our hearts and minds the same affirmative message that a physical touch does. Words can make us feel seen, heard, cared for. So I offer you these poems, with the hope that they will feel to you "as if a caress."

j.lewis

Table of Contents

fat rain

ask the fishes, massed in shrinking lakes
ask them what their wish is, what it takes
to give them elbow room. they answer:
fat rain

ask the firefighters, robed in soot
ask them what delights them, what would put
their minds at ease. they answer:
fat rain

ask the struggling farmers, planting seeds
ask them what would bless them, suit their needs
to make it through this drought. they answer:
fat rain

fat rain it is, then. rivers of rain
swirling, roiling atmospheric rivers
wringing themselves out like a million mops
over hills laid bare by fire,
lakes and streams run dry
reservoirs bled to nothing

fat rain to free the fishes
fat rain to counter fire
fat rain to end this drought
fat rain to put it out
fat rain after such dry times
fat rain, fat rain, fat rain

cancer woman

I am cancer woman
woman of cancerous things
dancing in your email
singing a siren song
my spelling as sloppy as
the soup in a hobo's cup

Cancer woman, my dear
prognosis as painful as
bare feet on hot coals
but I've got money, sir
money I can't use
and so I chose you

You, because you are
a godly man. Oh yes,
God told me so and said
smother that righteous soul
with your generosity
drown him in dollars

All I need, good and godly sir
is access to your bank account
so I can put the money in
and you can take the money out
right after you send me
just one thousand dollars
(American, please) to get
the transfer going. Going,

going, gone. And once again
in case I didn't reach your heart
I am cancer woman. Cancer.

the naming of things

the trouble with western medicine
said my thoughtful chinese friend
is the intense desire, the near obsession
with naming every problem

"back pain" is not enough to gnaw on
it must be infinitely more precise
like "progressive polyosteoarthritis
of the lumbar vertebrae"
that is a grand, definitive diagnosis

which doesn't change the nature of the pain
or the life story of an old man, bending
slowly, fighting his agony, just to pet his dog

but oh, the avenues it opens!
to have named it gives authority to blame
and opportunity to tame

never mind that the taming comes with a cost
every pill a poison that must be converted
by an aging liver, filtered by failing kidneys
or finding no success in alchemy
the curative knife and needle

name it, blame it, tame it, she said

and i suddenly wondered if that explained
our endless need to label those unlike us

salvation/damnation

i am awake, i am asleep
i am neither, i am both

lying in the naked heat
of grinding, dripping nights

i am dreaming, i am waking
i am neither, i am both

lying in the naked light
of fractured memories

i am smiling, i am crying
i am neither, i am both

lying in my naked heart
to friends and lovers past

ephemeral faces
forgotten names

i am living, i am dying
i am neither, i am both

lying in the naked curl
of fetal birth, of frozen joints

the swelling gift, the aging curse
of bone and muscle mocking

i am man, i am god
i am neither, i am both

lying in the naked arms
of impotence, omnipotence

yin, yang mystery
pleading for salvation

fearing for damnation
in this naked heat

help desk

in an unexpected
total role reversal
dad is on the phone
no one, says he
can get me online
so i called because i knew
you could walk me through it

i paused, surprised --
except for the familiar voice
i would have thought
it was a wrong number
but there he was
clear as sprint
asking advice
basic tech support

we talked
i walked him
through the installation
of dial-up networking
creation of a new account
stopping frequently
so he could catch up
biting my tongue
at his slowness
lack of experience

and wondered
how many times
he had done the same
when i was a stumbling child

warning: division by zero

okay, i know that's what the teacher said
but whose idea was that
to say that zero can be added to
subtracted from any number
no change to the number's value
or multiply and oh my
zero times any number and bam!
number reduced to nothing

but no dividing by zero
no way, no how, not ever-
undefined the teacher said
it doesn't mean anything

at which point my brain
went on its own side trip
digging up every phrase it knew
about division
and spit them back at me
divide and conquer
great divide
house divided
division of labor
infantry division
division of church and state
divide by zero - WAIT!

what happens if you divide
something by nothing

well, you get no division
the thing remains whole
undivided, intact
like a country indivisible
as in 'nothing can divide us'
nothing, as in zero, zip,
nada, zilch, nuttin'
can separate us

okay, teacher, i'm back
and you're not going to like this
but i just defined division by zero
and it's good, it's really good

bones of blue, eyes of gold

if i were to redefine myself
redesign everything from the inside out
i would start with bones of blue
not soft, gentle, pastels
but deep, intense, midnight blues
that hold the mysteries of the stars
the history of the universe
a place to hide my darkest thoughts
my deepest desires
bones to resonate like blues saxophone
vibrating their lowest tones right down
through the floor

someone else might want to make
muscles of coral, thousands of shades of red
but i want malachite, variegated greens
strength and beauty combined, sculpted

platinum is my preference for a heart
no corrosion, no soft parts to fail
or break at some hint of love lost
an enduring precious core, mi corazon

and so with other systems, the world's richest hues
a neon yellow brain, electrical circuits flashing
plumbing and pipes of fluorescent orange
circulating titanium white around and around and around
ending with eyes of purest gold so i could see through
deception and recognize goodness in everyone i meet

curves

i have loved from a distance
the arc of a raptor's beak
seen close up his bloody prey
whispered a silent thank you
for being too large to consider

i have loved from a distance
rolling, rippling hills
walked over crest, through trough
feeling more than hearing
the quiet yield of soil underfoot,
of leaves stirred in passing

i have loved from a distance
rhythmic, crashing waves
escaping the rounded ocean's
currents and tides to fall
breathless on receptive sand
their dying, curious foam
clinging to my naked feet

i have loved from a distance
winged things, and earth, and sea
measured them in my mind,
the weight of their beauty
resting there like a lover's breasts
in my cupped, quivering hands

i never cared for cats

or their ability to ignore me
until they wanted something
and then it was either
the plaintive mew, mew, mew
like sandpaper on my eardrums
or the claws-out climb
up my pant legs
so they could stare me
right in the face
with a self-centered
"well? where's dinner?"

they never learned either
from the sudden drop
back to the floor
that they had picked
the wrong post to scratch,
that the one they really wanted
was already in the kitchen
humming softly as she
made dinner for us all

but now the cat-bowl's empty
the kitchen's gone quiet
and the house is so large
that i'm thinking of something
i swore i'd never do
i'm seriously considering
getting myself a dog

driving in fog

the late hour vaguely remembered
the early rising, painful and slow

there's somewhere i must be—
a place, a person of importance

key to ignition is more reflex
than willful action

backing into the street
feeling my path to the highway
nothing is focused, nothing clear

visor a poor shield against
relentless morning sun
pulsing through the windshield

this is dangerous, i tell myself
madness multiplied by a million
driving through the fog in my brain

plus shipping and handling

i took you to the mail-stop store
bundled for winter in
polar-bear-white wrapping
with a bit of plain brown twine
just for security,
you know how i love that
extra touch, extra touch

counter man examined you
said nothing to me until he
placed you on the scale
where you were weighed
and not found wanting

one package north, insured
he said emphatically
that will be exactly twenty five
which was what i had
plus shipping and handling
which i did not

he stared at me absently
waiting for a dollar more
stared as i carried you
out the door and all the way
home where i debated gutting you
slitting the polar belly
to extract something superfluous

Echoes II

Blink, he said again.
It shouldn't take a genius
To figure out the obvious,
But I was seven then.

I knew it brought him pain
That my vision wasn't broader,
That I couldn't sense the order
In things he thought were plain.

I hadn't stopped to think
Today, when I berated
My small son. Belated
Echoes whispered, "Blink".

footsteps

did you do this thing
that boys all seem to do
walking behind a father
whose stride is longer
than his son is tall

tiny footprints waver
wander and stumble
then find the next depression
where father's weight
has pressed the soft ground
into his measured identity

did you laugh like i did
the day i realized that
as small as i still was
i could step from one print
to the next, no detours
no extra marks to mock me
for being insufficient

will you someday go searching
for your future in the tracks of the past

will you wear boots
or will you put on sandals
when that day of decision comes
that day when you set out
to walk in kisra's footsteps

an old familiar pain

morning's first alarm
with a backup
in case i fail to wake
open both eyes
try to stand

pain is my first awareness
head, neck, shoulder, hip
all the old familiar places
plus a new one
some muscle
bored with inactivity
spasms, cramps, squeezes
low moan from sleepy throat

agony fades and i realize
i have utterly forgotten
the absence of pain
cannot recall a soft dawn
when i stepped with grace
away from sleep, from dreams
into a new day's business
not a single memory
of a solitary step
that did not hurt

as if a caress

October's evening light as if a caress
soft brushing against my pain
whispers, as mother did then,
that the coming darkness
is not to be feared.

October's evening light as if a caress
lifts a quiet corner of night's quilt
draws it to rest on weary shoulders
shushes, as mother did then,
lullaby sung to its unchanging close.

October's evening light as if a caress
now only imagined, but eternally real,
dims day's demands and disappointments
invites, as mother did then,
my wrinkled, worried frown to sleep.

foxhunt

for Princess Diana

behind the inn
where the keeper reluctantly
supplies the hunt-master
and too many others
with their pre-hunt brandy
the dogs are restless
i can nearly hear the grinding
of three-day-empty stomachs
above the constant nervous barks
that only dogs understand

to one side stands a young man
holding a cage
where a hint of of red fur
and black snout betrays
the object of the coming chase -

he watches the milling
of canis and equis
and suddenly breaks
running for cover
thinking he can save her,
find a tunnel through to safety

the bugle sounds
the hounds, who have been teased
with a scrap of fox coat
howl and scramble over each other

in their eagerness to feed
they are fast
even in a pack
and the prey is soon in sight
the vixen's whimper
urges her protector on
but at the moment of freedom
at the tunnel's very mouth
she collides with fate
and as she dies
the hungry dogs swarm her
teeth flashing
cashing in
for the huntsman

hiding the truth

he painted a winding road into a distant perspective point
more watercolor than realism, details merely implied, but
always the promise that over every hill, around each bend
he would add another scene, the two of them moving
inseparably
through life's panorama

the last two years, he painted a lie along the center line
rich sunshine yellow. added clouds whose shapes
she failed to recognize, bright edges of deception over
a coquette sun, peeping, hiding

he knew his palette was running dry, but never shared
just mixed tears into the background wash to keep her
from the truth until the day he dropped lifeless brushes,
stranding her at the ragged edge of color, grief bleeding
off

        the

                page

mind the pets

if all my words cannot suffice
to wash away my own despair
what music could i ever use
to burn the sadness from your eyes

if we both drown beneath the depth
of your depression, unrelieved
who will mind the children, love
who will mind the pets?

bind up the brokenhearted

for Maman Laura (Joyce Mathison, MD)

our egocentric view of things
starts early enough
and lasts beyond useful bounds
to make us think somehow
of others as less fortunate
because they lack
whatever it is we hold
in abundance

and so we stepped into the fray
you to nigeria, me to a jail
ready to rescue, resuscitate
educate and operate
as though we alone
had anything to offer

we quickly learned
to check our egos
you in your baggage
me in my treatment cart
they were of no use
when sunrise to sundown
was filled with one purpose
serve, and serve again
until we were empty
sustained only by the spirit
of the great Healer

you were hampered by roads
or total lack thereof
me by the constant movement
the chaining and unchaining
the endless searches for contraband
your broken axles trumped my 'access denied'

we both learned humility
arrogance excised
perhaps by moist parental eyes
perhaps by the first-time mother
jailed and knowing she would lose
her swelling child

selfish interests were eradicated
by the antiseptic of a shy smile,
the touch of a tiny hand
the eyes that searched ours
asking why we would be so kind
when others turned away

those we thought we stooped to serve
vaccinated us against pride
infected us with their fierce love
exposed us to emotions
for which there is no cure, no escape

dopamine

he is not in the details
as i was often told
not smoking fiery red
no horns
no fork
no tail

no
the devil is in the dopamine
sliding into synapses
overriding receptors
interfering with the best intentions
afferent and efferent impulses
blocked, diverted, enhanced
as love and lust
motivation and addiction
adoration and adultery
swirl in sensual spirals
tiptoe through thoughts
dance across dreams

i am puppet to the stream
of chemicals flowing
never knowing
who controls the rails
on the mesolimbic line
is the engineer today
infernal or divine

preaching to the choir

mind you, i have been in choirs
large ones, small ones, good and ho-hum
and more than once, in church choirs

never in a choir loft, just
seats behind the podium
soft enough to nap in, but
don't let that happen

the sermon may be directed
at some other sinners, sure
but when it's time to rise and sing
you don't want to be the last one up
drowsy and dreamy and off pitch

more than once i've heard a preacher
shake his head, and say "i know—
i'm preaching to the choir" as if
his words meant nothing to anyone
or that the choir needed no repentance

but this i've learned, and it rings true
nothing sets the message on the congregation
like having the choir rise jubilantly
faces full of joy and conviction, songs
powerful and pointed and piercing
which is why it's always good
to preach to the choir, so the choir
will stand and sing

Broken-Toothed and Waiting for the Novocain

Isn't it just like my whole life's been?
Something breaks that I can't fix myself
And I end up waiting in one chair or another
Where the cure, though it promises relief
Always comes with its own measure of pain.

It was in high school, as I recall
When I fell in love with what's her name
Chased her mercilessly with poems, songs,
Anything I thought would bring her around

But when it came time for a field trip
Who's she sitting by on the bus?
Yep. My best friend. That was cruel,
Especially when he shrugged his shoulders

And mumbled "Well, she said she likes me,
What was I supposed to do?"
We're still friends. I don't know where
She ended up. It wasn't with him.

Broken heart, broken tooth, broken mind
They're all the same. Unfixable alone,
So you'll find me parked in some reclining chair
Broken-toothed and waiting for the Novocain.
Seriously, where's that Novocain?

blue moon in october

february, the virus
of no alleged concern

spring, the pandemic
shuttering lives

summer, the virus
seeking the unmasked

fall, the virus
reforged and surging

every day, the virus
blanketing the news

but did you see
last night, the moon?

did you see that moon?

Crotchety

I am turning into a crotchety old woman who talks to her cats and lives life on the page of a poem and I don't want any man's shoes under my bed or words in my heart wreaking havoc again.
(Auntie Em, 1997)

Have you noticed, he asks,
That woman in the house across
Who talks to her cats
As though they were human?
One day last summer
I heard her reading to them --
POETRY for heaven's sake,
And matching the rhythm of the verses
To the twitching of their tails.
Made my hair stand on end
And my spine run goosebumps.

Do you believe, I still recall
Exactly, every line?
Here, let me say it for you
It was meant to be repeated:

"Come kitty, kitty, kitty
Where art thou hiding now?
Art seeking mice, or scratching lice,
Or cleaning off thy brow?
If thou art under my bed yet,
I swear thee one time more,

There are no man's shoes there to find
Not there, nor by the door.
Come kitty, kitty, pretty please
And I will read thee verses
To free us from our wounded hearts
And broken love's harsh curses.
We are alone, dost thou not know
He'll ne'er to us come home?
Come sip this wine of words with me,
And let the bastard roam."

Does it make you shiver too?
She slammed the book shut,
Closed her eyes, leaned back
And said (I thought to ME),

"Well, did you like the poem, my dear?
Would you leave YOUR shoes lying,
Lying insincerely under a bed of LUST,
Let them gather the dust of broken dreams
While you carelessly break your pledges?
What hedges would you skulk behind,
What games of hide and seek
With her poor heart, poor heart.
He's torn mine all apart I fear,
Irreparable damage. Damn my age and immobility.
I close my eyes and see the gate
Swinging empty as he walked away
That day, that wretched afternoon.
To never love 'til kingdom come

Would be too soon. I rather prefer
Blood in my veins to his rhyming deceit."

She opened her eyes, saw me staring,
Shouted some obscenity
And drew the curtains.

disquiet

there is a building uneasiness
a sense of impending ending
with each announcement
of yet another famous death

at ages i once viewed as old
now younger than me by years
those departing and departed
whisper my name, though certainly
they never knew me

the rush of spirits rising
catches my breath away
half-tempting, half-mocking
the residue that i am
equally surprised and ashamed

that i have awakened again
earthbound and aging
worried i have stayed too long
praying that i may yet linger

for those roads that wait
beyond the crest of every hill
wooded trails and autumn gold
crashing waves and summer sand
the seductive breezes of spring

all these and more that flicker
and dim at each newly announced
"great loss to our world"
(whatever that world is to us)
these are the things of dark dreams
and my ever-growing disquiet

unfrozen in time

free from winter's prison
patient lilac bulbs
stir to life, stretching

dormant becomes vivant
drab slips into vibrant
pastel green of stem
dissolves to purple blossoms
offered gratis ad omnibus

roots wander from brown husks
white underground whiskers
that rise to emerald stalks
spring moving into summer

stick men

don't have shoulders, don't have hearts
or sleeves to wear them on either
don't have to worry about dress codes
or workouts for six-pack abs

don't have hair to style
or emotions to hide from scrutiny
don't have shoes to lace or tie
or teeth or smiles or frowns

don't have anything to prove
or anyone to prove things to
don't have arguments with friends
or jealousy or discontent

do have wives and children
i've seen them on car windows
do have stick pets too
who never need cleaning up after

don't have complicated lives to lead
or work, or debt, or age, or death
don't have much, yet represent
the simple complexity of
everything we are

erasing mistakes

for a crime scene cleaner
a message in crayon is nothing when you have
all the right solutions, it even comes out
of cracking wallpaper that
some cheap couple in a dirty trailer
used to blanket their pain
dress up their aching life together

the bathroom mirror was easiest
"*bastard*" went away in one simple wipe
hardly wrinkled the brawny towel
and just like that
a man he'd never met
was forgiven, sins wiped
sparkling clean

"*who is she*" made him stop to wonder
if "she" had been the town hooker
or the wife of someone he knew
he'd heard the rumors, they all had
a quick rub and then she too
was out of the story
erased from collective memory
onto a sponge he tossed in the trash

he had to leave "*i'll cut her throat*"
as a wave of unexpected nausea hit him
culmination of the blood, the smell,
the frustration and despair that had

soaked into this tiny space
too many uneasy nights
unsettled fights

recovering, that threat was gone with a firm swipe
every woman in the county breathing relief

fresh rags, brushes, water, soap
a spray of freshener in the kitchen
where he answered the question over the sink
"*if i hung myself, would you cut me down*"
by sawing through the waxy letters
with a rough cloth until the thought snapped
leaving frayed, bloody ends

job nearly done, the pressure of the place
weighing on his shoulders like a corpse
he frantically scrubbed the final, futile cry
from over her bed
"*i am gone*"
and so was he

full moon again

you would think
after more than fifty years
of regular monthly visits
the thrill would be
as b.b. king says "gone"
and yet

hanging full, plump, yellow
over the strait tonight
laughing through diaphanous clouds
throwing reflections on water
like veins of gold
i am awed again
with only one regret

no camera capable
of taking in the moving panorama
the subtle ascension
the illusion of trailing me home

spiders

she said a spider bit her
and she found it alive
trapped it under a clear glass
and started asking everyone
what is it, what is it

of course there's the fear
that it's somehow venomous
and then the finger falls off
but really, how many of those
spiders are there in your house,
in mine. i mean the killer types

the problem of course with spiders
is that if you say 'color' and 'size'
you've just identified not one
but several thousand suspects
none of whom have a single drop
of harmful spit to work with

but we round them up anyway
those who match the description
segregate them behind walls, under glass
fear and despise them all the same
because any one of them might be guilty
because there's a one in a million
chance of an accurate i.d.

aging children

why do songs last longest
longer even than the memory
of smells that call us home
my mother sang her mother's songs
as i sing hers to you
too small to join the chorus
but that will come

that will come
when time and growing spin you
make star trails in your sky
lullabies will fade to whatever
is popular at the moment
but in the isolated nights
always the little tunes

always the tunes
that cement you in place
along the branching scrawl
you will sing them to yourself
or to a budding leaf that you
yourself have molded
you age, it's true, but rhymes
and melodies do not

melodies do not leave us alone or lonely
like sap that ebbs in autumn
rises again in spring, the voiced
love that taught a hundred mothers past

will teach a thousand yet to come
as children come, and come of age
humming softly, and softly fade away

friends be like

i'll describe them the way i know them
old ones, true ones, new ones too

after years of knowing, sharing a conversation
with those forever-in-my-hearts still feels like

pulling up a reserved chair in the library
as the special collections curator hands me a book

i barely remember reading. the heading to each chapter
brings a flash flood of memories, good, bad, fuzzy, fun

each begging to be entertained, dusted off, examined
in the twin lights of your heart and mine

while others, more recent, are like the day mother took me
to a candy store, released my hand, and said "go, my treat"

samples all over the place had me running from case to case
tasting and begging for "a handful of this one", "a dozen of that"

never too full to gape, eyes and mouth alike
as undiscovered flavors teased my tongue

heart dust

it was accepted,
part of life -
the rain-resistant road
would never come by grandpa's door
spare him the occasional walk
ankle deep in mud
from highway to home -
summer sun on sand and clay
the closest substitution

foot or horse
car or tractor
each in passing raised
a greater or lesser cloud
the fine dust making us all
part of the earth
or the earth, part of us -
the dipper in the bucket by the well
a prize to the quickest

i keep a place in my mind
far away from everyone
separate, alone -
take willing walks
through muddy thoughts
to sit on the porch
scrap the shoes of my soul
free of the clinging earthiness
of every day

every tedious mundane morning
that sucks at my feet
that holds me back or down -

there too -
in seasons of sun
i run down rutted lanes
dirt packed, dry, and swirling
with the dust of a dozen summers
i have a thousand picture-thoughts
when you, like the well-bucket dipper
were my only ambition
and my thirsty solution

haying with tom

for a city boy, it is more
than amazing, more than
hard to comprehend
the length of the day
the merciless, necessary sun
but i opened the book
as tom opened the barn
he, knowing in detail
what the day held
me, ignorant of all
but the smell and weight
of baled hay. it had pulled
against my young hands
undeveloped muscles
pulled my father's face
into a rare smile as he reached
to heave the bale from pickup
to barn for later use. that
was all i knew when i climbed
on the mower with tom

climbed onto a day that stretched
forty pages into the future
forty acres into my imagination
where i felt my arms and back
stretch and knot, complain and
still obey through mowing,
raking, baling, storing

trip after trip from house
to field and house again
progress measured in flat-racks
filled and emptied
filled and emptied
until i lost count, though i knew
tom had not, knew that he
was counting what remained
in the field, even as the barn
filled, load by load

i was exhausted five pages in
but i had to stay, had to know
not the end of the story
but its middle, know the sear
of sun, the dusty hay-air
in my lungs, had to breathe it
with tom until i choked
and still hang on
i had to know what makes
men like him move through
days like this and sleep
and rise and do it again
and again this season
just like last and next

i would have cried, except
that in generations passed
men of my own family have done
this, and harder things, and in
the twisted helix they gave me

was the iron will to hurt
and move forward
ache and push on
and i did

clear to the last page and
after the last bale was lifted
stored in place, supper done
dust showered away
i whispered my quiet thanks
to tom for the explanation
the revelation of the strength
that is mine by lineage
the power built into my being
not just through my own pain and sweat
but through the patient daily perfection
of ancestors who would have loved to see
i follow their lead

mindfulness

soft crinkle of plastic as you
open a package of sourdough bread

tangy aroma that whispers
"you know me. you remember me."

resistance as you push down
the handle of the toaster until it clicks

muted crackles and pops as the toaster
comes to life. smell of burnt crumbs

loud crack as the sourdough pops up
sides unevenly browned, but perfect

curl of the butter as your knife
drags firmly across the surface

scrape, scrape, scrape of knife on toast
pale yellow of butter deepening as it melts

crisp crackle crunch of first bite
swirl of flavors on your tongue

contented sigh, wistful smile
acknowledgement that you eat alone

drugs and ear plugs

sandman doesn't stop here any more
no wave of the hand to scatter
the dust of dreams across her mind
no soft whispers to seduce her eyes
to close and let go the day

he has been replaced by newer magicians
diphenhydramine, acetaminophen
molded bits of waxy foam
black out curtains, or nearly so
heavier blankets and nightly routines
in search of r.e.m.

goodbye sounds like

when you are the passenger
no dash-mount panic handle
car and driver
taking the corner hard
hearing tires complain
in their own peculiar voice
shouting goodbye to pavement
soon to be abandoned

stomach tightens
and a frightened breath in
betrays you to the one
who grips your heart
hard like the steering wheel
and then
to emphasize the ride is over
raises both hands
and lets you go

the screeching screaming warning
of impending separation
takes so very long
to fade away

wallflower

fashions change with fickle frequency
but you always stay in tune
from the sassy egyptian wrap
that should have left men begging
to ride with you to the afterlife
to the black leather mini
that caused not one, but three
bent fenders with one little strut
across the avenue

but when it comes to dance
nobody cares, nobody dares
to single you out
fast song, slow song, mellow, ripe
you decorate the wall as
every girl around you steps out
on the floor to shake it
break it, press it, tease
come back at song-end with
a pouty, naughty smile and
that sideways look that asks
what's wrong with you, girl
what exactly is wrong

i see you, and i see me
watching the pretty poems,
the deep meanings
the gut-punchers being praised
paraded in review

spun around the floor
and coming back to rest
right beside me
with that same sideways look
that floats the question at me
what's wrong with your poetry, pal
what is wrong with you

though there was that one brief moment
when someone stopped to whisper
"hey, you're cute, too bad
i'm with somebody else"
neither of us blinked

your bird does not speak english

most mornings i am up and gone
long before the bird awakens
and begins her loud complaint
that you are still in bed

not up, not about, not crooning
not filling the food dish
not opening the cage to say
come out and play with me

but today's a holiday
and i hear the rising volume
of a cockatiel's complaint
at being ignored. the near
train-whistle panic that you
have simply walked out of the room
without her on your shoulder

also hear you fussing at her
telling her to shush, to wait
be patient, that life happens
on your time-table not hers
that you are in charge, the boss
the ultimate decider

i wince, hearing the echoes
of what i'm sure i said to you
when your speech was limited
to shrieks and chatter during

that pressured time in my life
when you, like your present pet,
did not speak english

When the Flavor Goes

If the DSM-V is just a fairy tale to you
or a labyrinthine mystery of symptoms
and you've never been endlessly sad
or anxious to the point of screaming
with nothing to be worried about, but still...

If you have been spared the agony of obsession
or the oppression of every waking moment fighting
just to dress and step out of your home
to a job that fills you with dread of mistakes
never made, but waiting behind every door

If SSRI and SNRI and Anxiolytics are words
that you'll need a dictionary or Google for
and stress-eating or hair-pulling are quirks
for other people, "crazy people"

Then think back to childhood when you knew
that any time you cried, you could rely on
those shiny little drops to taste like salt
and ask yourself this - just for compassion's sake
what would you do, if mental illness crushed you
so hard that even tears lost their flavor?

penny loafers

born in twenty-nine
nearly last in a line
of children that stretched
across that great depression
like a trans-continental railroad

by the time he started school
he was just a little slip
of a hungry boy, amazed
at how poverty pained and mocked him

shoes were never new but still, required
and when a sister's hand-me-downs
were the only things that fit his feet
then hand-me-downs it had to be

he gives a rueful smile
remembering how tough
he had to pretend to be
while all the better-off boys
in their sturdy leather cowboy boots
made him their daily target
the butt of every joke

he says it didn't matter
but his face tells the story otherwise
how else can a small boy rationalize
wearing penny loafers
without a single penny

San Francisco

I loved in San Francisco in the late 50's.
Never mind who, or why, or how long
or even how many. I lost count.
Edna would understand that, understand
the lone trees that in winter
bare their souls for careless birds.
Frost was there too. Close. Warm.
He loved cats, or so he said, then gave
the fog their feet to tiptoe in on.

Quiet. A luxury in that busy place,
defined not as the absence of noise
but of all human noise. The beach,
the waves, the sunsets from Alcatraz
burning that famous bridge, like
God burned a bush to make Moses stop
and listen. Just listen. The bush,
the bridge. Neither was consumed.

I loved in San Francisco. Deeply. Desperately,
but far too soon for the famous Summer,
the rebellion against the old guard.
Too early to pretend I was the one
who started it all.

On gray mornings when I felt no affection,
no connection to anyone around me,
I would stand alone on the Presidio cliffs
watching the morning mists obscure
the towers of the Golden Gate,
hide the passing of love.

regret is on the dessert menu

the descriptions are hyped, as always—
nothing actually tastes like heaven
or hell or sex on the beach
(and who's ever done that anyway?)
but someone got paid to write this
to make you want it, need it, badly

select carefully from the following regrets
you'll have a lifetime to live with your choice

"sweet regret"
simmered for decades in memory's tears
until every hint of sorrow
is reduced to caramel and cream.
you will forget you ever wanted
things to have been different

"regret flambé"
served as cold as revenge, surrounded
by a moat of bitter kirsch
ready to burn when you are

"regret serpentine"
your reptilian memories of 'could have been'
coiled around a mound of recollections
beautifully smooth, with an afterbite
to die for

"regret suprême"

all your heaviest secrets
bathed for years 'sous vide'
opened tonight at your request
drizzled with the distilled pain
you've kept so carefully inside
waiting for this moment to reveal

check up

i tell him i had covid almost a year ago
he nods and says yes, it's in my record

he asks what my concerns are, though that
is in the secure message i sent him days ago

we talk. or at least, i complain, he listens
easy fatigue, no stamina, vertigo, lack of focus

i thought he was listening, but he asks instead
about my depression and if the medication helps

yes, yes, i tell him, it works, but these symptoms
started long before the blues, so no. not that.

and then it starts. ekg, treadmill stress test
pulmonary function test, vials and vials of blood

every test, every sample, every result comes back
i'm in good shape for an old coot, and yet

the symptoms are still there. walk a block
in a mask and stop to huff, puff, and rest

climb one flight of stairs, pant for breath
nothing gets better, nothing gets easier

so what's an old geezer to do when the check up says
i'm fine, but my body disagrees. what's next?
what is coming next?

oh, england

a moment's noise, a flash, a bang
chaos wraps its flailing arms
around england's children
laughter modulates to screams
without changing key or cadence

run, run, anywhere there's space
stairway up, over, down
moths in frantic flight
pulled to flickering exit signs
safety, safety, where's my safety

the early news says there are parts
of the bomber, not the bomb
someone's son decided
he would rather die for his god
than live for humanity
destroy what he hated
rather than bury his hate
no courage to stand and face
supposed enemies
a faceless coward, deceived
into the false belief
that violence is the entry fee
to an imagined heaven

oh, england
tears again, and fear
mothers in anguish

dialing cells that won't respond
tonight or tomorrow
cells and owners both
endlessly out of service

six-eight time

slow and bluesy
i listen to the piano
lay the foundation
for the hungry voice
that whispers and wails
how she feels like a natural woman
and somehow it's my fault

i ignore her boastful lament
concentrate on the chords
tonic
dominant seventh
walk the bass down
modulate
i think i have it
and the keys under my fingers
reluctantly agree

singers are never in short supply
and one who has loitered
outside the door of my practice room
is happy to provide the voice
in fact already knows the words
the emphasis and pauses
that make this piece thrill me
i shiver as she ends soft and low

the conversation after
leads somehow to dance

she claims the meter of a song
can just pick you up
and slam-dunk drop you in love
with whomever you're with at the time
wants to demonstrate
so the needle meets the vinyl
sets the bluesy piano off again
she slips her arms around me
begins to move in six-eight time
and there i am in love
forever
or at least
until the song ends
and i don't even know her name

for the birds

the dove of peace
alleged to be pure white,
a sign of heavenly approval
i've never seen in person

but i have heard
mourning doves calling
early in the dark morning
late in the nebulous night
and i wondered
if peace and sorrow
might be more connected
than i had imagined

the bluebird of happiness
could be any species
with the right coloration -
scrub jay, parakeet, other
but i've always pictured it
a western bluebird
small, precious, and always
out of reach

but last night in a dream
the hummingbird of healing
flitted about my head
and as i stilled mind, body, breath
it darted about, perching
on an ear, a shoulder, a hand -

a soundless vision that hovered
touched, then looked at me
yes, *looked at me*
for a demi-second, an eternity
then vanished in a flash of color

on waking, i remembered
every wing beat, every touch
of a tiny talon that left
an unexpected sense of wholeness
of happiness, of peace

dreams, i whispered to no one,
dreams are for the birds

how to make love

a beginner's list

step one:
start with a simple question
meant only for yourself-
what is it that attracts me so
exclude all physical references
(because parts are parts
and everyone has them)
find that answer and hold it carefully
so it doesn't bruise or break or fly away

step two:
another self-query-
what would my heart feel
if i put my hand on her cheek
brushed her hair back and watched
her eyes half-close
her lips part in a rising smile
pray that the answer is more than
nothing

step three:
place her hand over your heart
so she knows she doesn't need to ask
or answer anything
let it rest there until she steps closer
puts her arms around you

step four:
put this list away
it has served its purpose
use it only if you wake one day
and find you've lost the answers

first words

every child born speaks the same language
in varying tones of screams and cries
for reasons we guess at darkly
when calm, they make random vowel tones
not round and full like opera
but soft, like romeo behind the roses

we wait, we talk, we wait for them
to learn the sounds we want to hear
coax and cajole until we end up
sounding more like babies than babies
clapping and beaming when something
remotely approaching 'da da'
slips out of a tiny face

but what path in life might be marked
by taking that newly born child
and rather than cooing and clucking
whispering into a miniscule ear
the name of your God, followed by
the child's name
and if you wish, your own

unstrung

when the day ends
pulls a shade down
on the sun of all you are
i will play your song
and then
put my guitar to rest
each silver string released
tucked away
in coils of remembering
and i will wait
find ways to pass the time
without the music
of you with me

when the day comes
that you go
and leave me
all unstrung

walking in fog

that time of year has come again
when one morning you awaken
to a world shrouded in mist
the clouds of heaven come down
to filter out the background noise

you look outside,
noon dimmer than twilight
streetlights still on to say
you need us now, we will stay
as long as the sun is covered

down the sidewalk, wet with dew
your neighbor fades to gray
and then to nothing. you know
she's going somewhere familiar
some everyday place you also know
and yet, in the swirling cloud
of a winter day, not every path
is fully visible

you think of your aging father
who called last night to talk
and got lost in the mists
of memory, wandering down streets
and alleys and roads no longer used
no lamplights left to guide him
down paths he once knew
no longer fully visible

off the deep end

so the cycle goes like this:

1.
do something stupid, anything
sell some meth, use some dope
ride your bicycle while [insert race]
talk to yourself and say weird shit
scare people at the grocery store
who promptly call "the popo"

2.
get arrested, booked, jailed
often while still too high
to remember any of the meds
you are supposed to take daily
to keep this from happening

3.
sober up, demand to know why your meds
(the ones you couldn't remember)
haven't been started yet, because
a jail is supposed to know everything
about you, including your health history
even if you've never been there before

4.
realize how messed up you are once sober
suck up to the mental health staff, begging
for "the good stuff", which you know isn't coming

drop into your infantile behavior, as if it helps
and there you are: kicking and banging and going
off the deep end, until you take what actually works

5.

mellow out, calm down, go to court, get released
or stay a while longer, try to behave
until you get sprung back to the streets
where instead of picking up your two weeks
supply of medication and making an appointment
you cycle back to 1, and go around again

peddlers

making the circuit, stops in towns
large and small, they played them all
in wagons with billboard sides

announcing with a flourish that here
here was the total cure for every ache
physical, mental, emotional, imagined

top hat as like as not, sometimes a cane
and frequently, a lovely assistant
more shapely than a potion bottle

hired to display his wares and hers
sequins and smiles for the gents
knowing nods for the ladies

some say there was alcohol involved
probably true - what solvent more suitable
for various nefarious ingredients

jump to the twenty-first century
the wagons are gone, the restless crowds
the hat, the cane, the girl — all gone

replaced with screens large and small,
every household a target for the latest cures
no more snake oil, no sir. now they're selling
fish oil and folate and fluoxetine

grindstone

some nights i think too much
so my ego turns to powder
like dried corn
caught between
mortar and pestle
as i grind against
the inconsistency
of all i want to be
of all i am

a new blessing

count the sand along the beach
any beach will do
and tell me if that number
comes close to the constant dread
that this new child
like the last one
will not really live

count the hours, minutes, seconds
when fear suddenly flares
without warning, without reason
without fail
yet she holds fast to hope
lets the waves of anxiety
roll back into the deeper ocean
of what she has endured
building a sea wall with her faith
holding back the daily doubts

count the day of delivery
as the first of many to come
the whirlpool of activity around her
as those who know how
comfort and prepare her for triumph
for a shout into the sea-laced wind
new life! new life!

count my posterity
and rejoice with me, aloud

join your hands with mine
to lift this infant woman

heavenward whence she comes
to beg of God a blessing
on her head
and on her house

creation songs

before there was earth to walk on
before the salted sea rushed
its brushed jazz rhythm against the shore
long before wind came sniffing
across the bamboo forest, searching
for the soft vibration of hollow tubes
music pulsed through the universe
pervasive and pregnant with possibility

when the earth grew round past containing
when it birthed every creature
groaning and spitting fire
beneath the labored pain
music whispered to the heaving globe
calming and quieting the bright flows
shushed the bellowing, trumpeting calls
of new born life, lulled them to rest

every creature knows those birth songs
chants them for each new generation
teaches all young things to listen
to the call of creation

but oh, the special gift to those
who have hands to hold, lips to breathe
across a hollow reed, a dried bone flute
releasing the haunting melodies
of first music, first lullaby, first birth

gold pen

george is gone for good they say
did his thirty years and retired
didn't complain much either
about having nothing to do
after, i mean

george was made to stand up
walk to the front of the room
shake the hand of the c.e.o.
and smile like he meant it
and say a word to two

he made it just two: "*thank you*"
as they handed him his prize
for hard work, for dedication
for not making their jobs harder

it was a finely crafted thing
that lay gleaming in a walnut box
it looked so fine, so fancy
that george cracked a real grin
though all of us knew
he really doesn't write much

me, i've got another five years
before i catch up with george
and having watched the show once
i am convinced of this, for certain
i could do without the ceremony
but I sure would like that pen

choosing a path

chicken bones tossed
by fingers as thin as they

tea leaves stirred
settling in a thin ceramic cup

slips of paper in a bowl
shaken and selected

words scratched in frost
losers erased by boot tip

pattern of birds in flight
at first light of day

mindful meditation
the spirit manifesting

all paths lead to this
knot in the calendar

and lead away to unknown joys,
unwanted sorrows

tomorrows chosen
by today's first careful steps

neural fury

across the plasmoid chasm
membrane shrouded forces marshal
swirling in their eagerness
to jump the gap
be swallowed in the mystery
of the other side

unruly, they break across
spinning, leaping, soaring—
the fury of a solar flare unleashed
spikes into the opposite wall
unbidden, unwelcome, unhindered
pulsing exuberance
into unsuspecting muscles

i watch, helpless
as giles de tourette
plays havoc with my son

evening prayers

this is my nightly ritual—
to bow my head, kneel
beside my bed and then
from a growing list
begin my pleading

so many broken hearts
and failing bodies to worry over,
people i love and others
i barely know but who have whispered
"pray for me, please?"

and so i do, i do, though i know full well
that some will heal and some will not
it isn't up to me—
i never know who's in which lucky group
and whether the ones who stay
or the ones who go are most blessed

in the end, maybe
it isn't about them at all
maybe it's about finding
soft places in my heart
where asking for a friend
whose sister is suddenly ill
or the inmate whose mother just died
and will be buried without him,

maybe it's that sweet compassion
that matters most, and why
these evening prayers must
never lose their breath

in the other direction, a rainbow

the wind is from the west again
not the howling of a hurricane
nor the whisper of a lover's breath
but bold and purposeful
a woman with something on her mind

chasing her, and caught up
in the strength of her resolve
come clouds, dark and pregnant
with rain, with pain, with blessing

and in the other direction
arcing across the sunlit afternoon
full of promise and legend and seduction
there for my delight, if only for this hour

stretching from earth to sky
no clear beginning or ending
just a soft fade of brilliant colors
that holds the promise of us, reunited

Bless Us, Lord

Oh, bless us, Lord
to see beyond
our Catholic confessions
our Protestant pride
our Mormon murmurings
May we be blessed!

Oh, bless us, Lord
to reach beyond
our selfish souls
our fragile fears
our silent sorrows
May we be blessed!

Oh, bless us, Lord
to care beyond
our Sunday sermons
our Friday feasts
our weekday worries
May we be blessed!

Oh, bless us, Lord
to move beyond
our insolent idolatry
our boastful bigotry
our terrible treachery
May we be blessed!

Oh, bless us, Lord
to feel beyond
our hedonist hearts
our venomous vanity
our careless condemnations
May we be blessed!

Oh, bless us, Lord
Oh, change our hearts
Oh, may we be so blessed!

questions from the young monk

when there is no answer
what is the point of the question?

the young monk asked

~~

when an old monk and a young monk
walk together do they become
the same age?

the young monk asked

~~

if the purpose of life
is to find your purpose in life

is this not a circle
with no end?

the young monk asked

~~

when silence says more than words
why do we continue speaking?

the young monk asked

~~

gallup winter

since the first insult
of taking land was not enough
alcohol was added to the stew
that western europe offered
original americans

i came much later to the scene
learned just enough history
to know of the long walk that
stripped the remnants of pride
from the navajo nation

replaced it with welfare
boarding schools
and pawn shops that would loan
just enough for another round
of stupor

that was the backdrop
to one of the harshest winters
anyone in gallup remembers
when the bitter cold wind
sliced through even the thinnest cracks
and johnny yazzie's levi jacket
was nowhere near enough

list of denials

first
i never loved you
not in any way that would last
for less than this life
and into the next

second
you cannot depend on me
for anything beyond the basics
as we've discussed so many times
"having food and raiment,
let us be content therewith"
just call everything else i give
gravy, frosting, excess

third
i don't enjoy
being around you much
for anything other than
the hiking, kayaking, picture taking,
movies, shopping, impromptu dates,
quiet snuggling, and other things.
or the food. oh, the food.

fourth
i simply don't want to marry you
at least not again in this life
because that would involve
separating the entity known as 'us'

dividing the conjoined twins
that you and i have become
just to re-attach the two parts
and that would make no sense
no sense at all

last
if you should ever tell
someone, anyone, everyone
about this little list
i will deny that i meant
any of it as jest
it's best you leave it
alone

seven at one blow

in fable, it was nothing more than flies
useless pests to us, foul little insects
getting into everything we love
our food, our homes, our ears
until we wanted to scream
and then the tailor, fed up
lets go a mighty blow and there
seven ugly corpses in one felling

in life, it seems that friends, like flies
are dropping, falling, giving one last
desperate buzz of their earthly wings
then quiet, deathly quiet, eternally still

but will we make of God a tailor
who strikes willy-nilly at our dearest ones,
taking no more thought of them
than bothersome insects, breeding
and crawling around His footstool?

oh, never is it so, never so
for God, who is our Father,
He who notes every sparrow's fall
with His own heavenly tears
surely grieves for us, knowing
how deeply we mourn what we see
as loss, deprivation, and pain
blocked by our own misty eyes
from seeing the glory they go to

it takes so long to learn
not to live without them
but to live with the memory
of love, of laughter, of life
let us not forget—they are not dead,
but sleep in Christ, ready to meet us
in a coming year

beggar's whisper

enough
enough
less statement than plea
eyes to heaven beg release

the load has been lifted
shifted, shared
through every option,
yet persists -
heavy oppressive relentless burden
too much to bear
too little to smother the pain.

again the whispered litany
frail against the trailing wake
of dust in the afternoon sun
enough
enough
enough

And If I Dream - II

Some fear and some, unquestioning, desire
that undiscovered country from whose bourn
no traveler returns. They halt or haste
to dreams they do not know--a desert waste
or sweet oasis waiting in its turn,
celestial burnings or damnation's fire.

I feel no fear, sense no undue attraction
to that land, that world of rumored night.
And when I make that pilgrimage at last,
what dreams may come will never be surpassed
by any colors bolder or more bright
than those created by our long affection.

The brush and oils borrowed from the days
of you and I, our pleasure and our pain,
will paint the details of a quiet glance,
a look, a touch, a slow and passioned dance
for all to see. The closeness that we gain
through love, encanvassed there, forever stays.

how to seduce a poet

if the poet is male—
show up wearing nothing
except a dust cover
slick and colorful
let it drop to the floor

flutter a page or two
as though eyelashes
were kissing his fingertips
exhale the scent
of printer's ink
and leather binding
intoxicate him
but not too much
or too soon

once you have his attention
(and trust me, you do)
invite him to open the cover
run his hand down
the title page

and done - he is yours
completely. he will
be awake all night

~

if the poet is female—
try showing up in softback
nothing to prove

no explanations
turn so she can read
the rear jacket testimonials
see what makes you
worth perusing
worth pursuing

quote, if you will
an intimate poem
pull something from millay
hinting that you'll remember
every kiss, even if edna
did not, that you know
nothing of forgetting
midnight cries

lay her hand gently
on the abstract cover
art that speaks
of mystery
of possibility

draw her in with
the first verse
unassuming, unafraid
be vulnerable, be brave
knowing that her eyes
will open wide
at the words tattooed
along your spine

slip her a folded note
that says 'i left a review...'
her resistance is gone

for either—
recite the final verse
of your latest poem
without explanation

without apology
for what came before

leave what comes after
to imagination

at work we never talk of war

there is so much happening
every minute of every day
someone having a crisis
or causing a catastrophe

the radio shouts at us
"mental health, call quad C"
"mental health, i have one
threatening to kill himself"
"mental health... mental health..."

i don't dare announce that
i'm on my lunch break because
that would be callous, so
i respond while my lunch cools
thinking that even if it costs
my employers an extra hour of time
it has to be done, food can wait

we chart mostly in silence
until i can't handle the quiet
and dial up some blues on youtube
anything to keep me from getting
too wrapped up in solving problems—
that would come at my own expense
the final minutes of the day
slip by and the time clock chimes
as i swipe my badge to prove i was there

only when i am outside again
and the blue sky over yellow anything
pulls me back to ukraine's fields
news updating by the minute it seems
convoys and sanctions and SWIFT
and EU and NATO and Switzerland
breaking its neutrality
it's all right there in my face,
in my ears, in my thoughts, my heart

but at work we never talk of war
how could we with so many
broken minds to try and save

holding you

on the day you took your first breath
i cradled your smallness in my arms
filled with wonder, hope, expectation

on the day you took your first step
your tiny hand held my little finger
uncertain, curious, and bold

on the night of your first bad dream
i sat on your bed, unspeaking
holding you in the darkness

on the day you drove your first car
the night you got your first kiss
the day you left home for good

and every other first for you
i held you as close as i dared
wanting to hold you up, not back

on the day that i heard of your latest first
i knew there was nothing more to do
than to hold you in the light
just hold you in the light

my mother's seasons

winter was her childhood
spring her early escape
from the disaster of two parents
fueled by liquor
She married much too young
but the choice was freedom
or return to the daily terror

summer was painfully long
full of children and worry
music and love

as children grew
so did she into full bloom
her fruitful life evident
at every turn

but seasons pass
cannot be postponed

an early harvest by
the grimmest of reapers
left fruit boxes empty
malignancy without mercy
her quiet summer's end

all dressed up to go

the parking lot is early-dark
but i am here, hungry
staring at the puzzled face
receptionist's frustrated fingers
searching for some hint
of my medical past

i feel a muted belly-rumble
reminder of that single scoop
my after-midnight sin
asking for his twin
interrupted by she-who-must-be-paid
no matter the outcome

i have inhaled this air before
stale with hints of anesthesia
and disinfectant wipes
warmed these chairs for strangers
thankless and preoccupied
with their own impending stories

the irony of being billed
by a system that can't find me
brings a brief smile
cut short by the summons
to gown and robe as though
i were a king and this—
this is coronation day

helpful hands guide mine
as i fumble with the over and under
feeling four again, laughing
at the tangled ties

maroon socks
with non-slip rubber stripes
painted carefully on each bottom
and i am ready to present

except that the court cutter
that clown of a surgeon
has forgotten the date
left papers unsigned

and like the babe in bethlehem
there is no room in this inn
not even for one who has paid
reservations in advance

what can i do but sigh
surrender my regal attire
walk softly out the sliding doors
skip happily to the ice-cream store
all dressed up and more than ready to go

Tonight I Will Make Soup

Starting, as my mother would
with nothing more than water
and a heart full of worry
for more than one child
struggling to stay afloat.

Tonight I will make soup,
but don't expect chicken
for the sappy soul.
I will add garlic, coriander,
and a cup of quiet contemplation—
ingredients I've learned to treasure
for their depth and breadth of flavor.

Quiet most of all, nothing
but the sound of a full rolling boil.
Full silence as vegetables, beef,
and rice slide into the waiting water,
tamping the turbulence.

Tonight I will make soup
naming aloud each child of mine
letting the swirl that trails
behind the stirring spoon
absorb and dissipate my fear,
knowing that this soup
will bring them home
where they are loved.

encore

come back into my life old friend
center stage and spotlight
sparkling as you spin
inspiration winking
from your sequins
and your smiles

come out from the curtained shadows
that hold you in brooding silence
always present and ever absent
tip your hat and tap your cane
bow with me again
as we do the old soft-shoe

don't let this show
close down

new chairs

i didn't expect white
but i knew black was out
maybe natural wood

anything to replace
the worn out and breaking
cane-bottomed kitchen chairs

chairs that had lasted
far beyond expectation
holding on, like me. holding on

when she found new chairs
online, of course, she said
these are the ones, but

you will have to assemble them
and i thought to myself
i've put so many things together

what's four more chairs
prefab and requiring only a
screwdriver and included wrench

done in no time, and the old chairs,
faithful to the end, were cut apart
to fit the garbage can

no funeral, no eulogy, and almost
no regret, except for a twinge
as i sawed through the last leg

wondering what might become of me
when i am old past usefulness
but not ready to give in

somewhere in the pause

there is meaning
unspoken of course
leading me to an
uneasy anticipation
of what is to come-
longed for pleasure
or dreaded pain, again

the button is released
and the train continues
though down a different track
i am certain of that much
leaving me at the station
unresolved and unsure
whether i have been teased
by a silent invitation
or spared an elegant execution

aching

beginning with lines from "Holiday Concert"
by Maryann Corbett

for years, he will wince at the thought
of singing, yet will ache to sing
but never quite enough to try again
another talent stillborn in the audible
amusement of grown-ups who have spent
so many years burying their own aches
that they no longer remember
how deep it drills
how long it lasts

he will ache in awkward moments
holding hands, a first fumbling kiss
when everything he feels begs to rise
like pavarotti and fill the sky
mounting above high c and to the stars
but he will not, he cannot risk
the possibility of hearing his voice
his once innocent voice shatter his dreams
splatter his ego across the dingy stage
of adolescence where every attempt to sing
is a disaster waiting its entrance cue

i've never made a pilgrimage

to anywhere, for any reason
not to any place marked as holy
searching for some residue
of righteousness to inhale

not that there's any lack
of things i'd like to see—
the upward steps of mont st michel
taking me closer to heaven

the bethesda pool that angels stirred
infusing the water with healing
for the first, but only the first
who managed to slip in quickly

such things for me are history
a physical confirmation of what was,
of ancient events that did not
include me, but might have

none of them mean more
than walking in a quiet summer forest
thick with the reverence of redwoods
whose rich tenacious lives endure

the whisper and roar of breakers
along a deserted beach where
sitting alone in the sand
i am everything and nothing

the heady perfume of cherry blossoms
thick on springtime branches
or the flash of a perseid meteor
across an ebony sky

none of these, though marvelous,
are any more sacred than this:
a quiet hour of meditation
on all who've touched my life

he is not here

the holy canon asserts
that "thou shalt cry,
and he shall say,
Here am I" but that is
a promise bound to performance
and in the failure to act
we are often left calling, calling
with the sinking realization
that he is not here

he has not broken faith with us
our conscience burns within
accusing, replaying perfectly
how far we have gone away from him
what sins have separated us
from heaven like ice floes
moved by subtle currents
daily diminished until gone

unless we summon winds of repentance
to push us against the tide
against the constant commotion
of worldliness that swirls around us
wind as from angel wings
that whispers us to safe harbor
where the smallest plea is answered
with the greatest of gifts
as God himself assures us
here am I

have a blessed day

junkie, joker, con-man, thief
parade of ailments large and small
daily sameness interspersed
with moments of intervention
the kind that saves a life
at least for now

and in the least expected moments
on a single, weary day
surprising phrases reprised
not by the healer, the giver
but by the grateful takers
who bring their simple ills
to his feet
and parting
offer him a respite from it all
have a nice day
have a blessed day
god bless you
blessings on you
blessings

ACKNOWLEDGEMENTS

POEMS PREVIOUSLY PUBLISHED IN COLLECTIONS

a clear day in october, Empire & Great Jones Little Press (2016)

"aging children", "Crotchety", "dopamine", "goodbye sounds like", "neural fury", "six-eight time", "unstrung"

every evening is december, Praxis Magazine Online (2019)

"Bless Us, Lord", "hiding the truth", "salvation/damnation", "warning: division by zero"

do you hear it?, Kelsay Books (2020)

"drugs and ear plugs"

leave a light on, Cyberwit Press (2021)

"San Francisco", "the naming of things", "your bird does not speak English", "evening prayers"

POEMS PREVIOUSLY PUBLISHED INDIVIDUALLY

Inwood Indiana, "bones of blue, eyes of gold"
Spire Light, "gold pen"
Lothlorien Poetry Journal , "how to seduce a poet", "regret is on the dessert menu"
The Song Is , "i never cared for cats"
Whispers , "list of denials"
Agape Review , "preaching to the choir"
Verse-Virtual , "cancer woman", "penny loafers", "plus shipping and handling"

Jim Lewis (j.lewis) is the Editor of Verse-Virtual, an online poetry journal and community. He has been writing most of his life, primarily poetry.

When he isn't working or writing, he enjoys playing piano and guitar, singing, kayaking, and photography.

Previous publications

Collections

a clear day in october E&GJ Little Press, 2016

do you hear it?, Kelsay Books, 2020

leave a light on, Cyberwit Press, 2021

Chapbooks

every evening is december, Praxis Magazine, 2018

in the shadow of the ark, Self-published

the plagues, Self-published

april with friends, Self-published

december gifts, Self-published

www.ingramcontent.com/pod-product-compliance
Lightning Source LLC
Chambersburg PA
CBHW022158160726
48282CB00024B/235
* 9 7 8 8 1 8 2 5 3 9 1 0 5 *